WORKING WITH
ZODIAC ANGELS

A White Eagle meditation workbook

Contents

WORKING WITH ZODIAC ANGELS

A White Eagle meditation workbook

THE WHITE EAGLE PUBLISHING TRUST
LISS . HAMPSHIRE . ENGLAND

www.whiteaglepublishing.org • www.whiteagle.org • www.thestarlink.net

Introduction
by Jenny Dent

Since ancient times, astrology has been a part of 'wisdom school' instruction, as has been understanding of the work of angels and the part they play in human life. It has always been a part of the spiritual unfoldment path offered to followers of White Eagle's teaching.

This workbook pioneers the bringing together of astrological understanding and the inner meaning of the zodiac signs, with knowledge of the great angels working on the vibration of each sign. My mother, Joan Hodgson, founder of the present day WHITE EAGLE SCHOOL OF ASTROLOGY, laid the foundations for this work in her two books WISDOM IN THE STARS and ASTROLOGY THE SACRED SCIENCE. Throughout the writing and compilation of both this workbook and the Zodiac Angel Cards (see p159), those involved have been very aware of Joan's loving and encouraging presence.

This book is the result of a group working together, each bringing their individual skills to the project. Originally written by me, it has arisen out of the work I have been doing with groups of students in the White Eagle Lodge, both those already involved in the White Eagle path of service, and those coming for the first time to a White Eagle Retreat Day. My 'Working With Your Zodiac Angel' Days led to our Zodiac Angel Cards, mentioned previously, which have become a White Eagle Publishing Trust best-selling item.

This workbook can be used in conjunction with the Zodiac Angel cards, or quite separately. Both are brought to life by the inspiring angel images originally conceived and painted by Annie Woods. These have been given their colour tones, linking with the energy of each element and zodiac sign, by my colleague Anna Hayward, who has been responsible for the overall design of both the cards and workbook. Both bring together—in a unique way—angels and astrology, and form unique publications in this present day—though they are deeply impressed by the knowledge of wise teachers of the ancient past.

And...like a golden thread, White Eagle's wise words shine light throughout this book...listen to him speaking to your inner self...

We offer this book to you with love and encouragement.

WORKING WITH ZODIAC ANGELS

This workbook can be an accompaniment on a journey through the zodiac during which you can discover ways to attune yourself to the beautiful zodiac angels. Each sign of the zodiac has a particular angel of its own which can help us develop unique qualities and each angel has an affinity with one of the elements (earth, air, fire, water).

The book can be used in several ways: as a daily, monthly or seasonal journal as well as a place to record all your thoughts, meditations, aspirations and affirmations. This is a workbook for everyone, whether you have astrological knowledge or not. It can be used any way you wish, but below there are some suggestions for ways in which you might start.

The CD comprises an introduction to a meditation for each one of the twelve signs that will help you with your attunement to the fundamental vibration of each angel and increase your awareness of the presence and guidance of angels within your life.

The twelve zodiac signs are divided between the four elements; Fire, Earth, Air and Water.

Each of these elements can manifest in three qualities: Cardinal, Fixed, Mutable.

	AIR	WATER	FIRE	EARTH
CARDINAL	Libra	Cancer	Aries	Capricorn
MUTABLE	Gemini	Pisces	Sagittarius	Virgo
FIXED	Aquarius	Scorpio	Leo	Taurus

Suggestions for using the workbook

1. Using the chart, find the element related to your zodiac sign. Contemplate the key words, practice the meditation given and use the affirmations; this will help you to immerse yourself in the essence of the element.
2. Find the quality of your zodiac sign, read about that quality, again use the meditations and affirmations; this will help you to become absorbed in the essence of this quality.
3. Use the affirmations, teaching and meditation suggestions for your sign of the zodiac—your sun sign.

Further Activities

When you have completed this and feel ready to move on, you might like to consider the other two zodiac signs associated with the same element and tune in to the subtle differences in each vibration which the element brings to you.

You could also investigate the three other signs of the same quality and explore and feel their unique vibrations.

Now perhaps you would like to consider those signs, elements and qualities which you have not yet worked with so that you are completing the zodiac and the circle.

The Astrological Temple

The Astrological Temple Meditation at the end of the book will bring inspiration to your explorations. Visit it at any time; this will support and encourage you on your journey of attunement to the angels of the zodiac.

FIRE

Angels of the FIRE element bring with them a very beautiful vibration of God's glorious unconditional love. They help awaken greater LOVE in the human heart.

The deep soul lesson of the fire element is LOVE, an absolutely unconditional love in which there is no room for narrow, rigid perspective or judgement.

Visualise the way in which flames can consume all that is old and unwanted, making way for the new. This is how this element can function.

These angels bring a strong feeling of life and vitality, of moving forward and awakening greater creativity. They inspire, warm, 'light up' and re-energise the whole being of all who come into their aura.

Using the affirmations which follow helps bring an awareness of these angels:

> Every cell of my being radiates love.
>
> The bright flame of God's love shines within me.
>
> Unconditional love surrounds and supports me.
>
> The creative fire of love inspires me.

Key Words to help focus attunement to the angelic Fire vibration

Stimulating   Cleansing   Loving   Inspiring   Radiant   Consuming   Transforming

Fire Angelic Qualities

Power, Vibrancy, Vigour, Unconditional Love, Miracle Working

Key Saying:

'When the fire element in the soul burns as a clear bright flame through a cleansed physical body,
such a soul becomes a natural healer, consoler and inspirer of others.
The soul which has endured the fires of suffering grows in inner strength
so that the inner light of divine love can be directed with great power.
This soul now begins to understand the secrets of the white magic.'

Joan Hodgson

As you attune to this energy, write down any affirmations of your own and use the following pages to record your own
notes and meditations.

'The human spirit is a spark of the Divine Fire, unconscious Godliness, breathed forth to grow
into a conscious God-being.'

7

'May your heart be quickened with the fire of love.'

'Your eyes being illumined, touched with the Divine Light, you see the beauty of all things.'

'May you be caught up in the fire of the love of the angels.'

'Receive the baptism of holy fire, and you will be illumined with the wisdom of the spirit.'

'Fire, the purifier—will draw all life back again to itself,
then there will be reborn the divine fire, in *you*.'

'Fire is the creative power.'

EARTH

Angels of the EARTH element bring a feeling of strength and connection with nature and all forms of creation. . all creatures. . all plant life. . the earth herself. . rocks, minerals, crystals. . .

They help to awaken in the human heart an awareness of the inter-connectedness of all life forms. . .

They awaken in the mind and heart an aspiration to serve and care for all human life. . .

All life is created by the Father-Mother God and the angels are the messengers and co-workers who work with the Creator to bring into being the infinite variety of physical form we experience on earth.

Using the affirmations which follow can bring an awareness of these angels:

> I am unique, yet one with all created life.
>
> I am a channel for God's healing light.
>
> I have courage and am strong to serve.
>
> I am grounded and balanced materially and spiritually.

Key Words to help focus attunement to the angelic Earth vibration

Strong Steady Sensible Established Maintained Physical
Mighty Foundation-Laying Serving Nurturing

Earth Angelic Qualities

Strength Power Glory Intricacy Beauty Vastness Stillness

Key Saying:

'Think of spiritual evolution as a most perfect procedure. . .
all the pieces and broken fragments of life are used
and brought together in an indescribably lovely way
to perfect the pattern of man's life on earth.'

White Eagle

'The earth is not dark as you suppose, but is full of fire and light!'

'The sense of smell is related to the element of Earth.
You can smell the essence of life, the inner vibration.'

'Saturn is the planet of Light, of illumination. Saturn is the great teacher of the Earth.'

18   'After illumination, the soul has to use the power of the divine fire to control physical matter.'

'In the Earth Initiation the individual has to learn that all substance is God.'

'The Earth Initiation teaches the soul to free itself from limitation
and that there is no such thing as death.'

'Your true state of embodiment is in the eternal light.'

AIR

Angels of the AIR element are closely linked with the mental plane and the thoughts of all humankind. They can touch human minds with divine wisdom and a much deeper intuitive awareness of the brotherhood of all creation.

Air angels can awaken truer understanding of the unity of all life and bring about greater tolerance one for another. Attuning to their influence can be really helpful when seeking greater wisdom and understanding of life's many challenges. The breath is a universal aid to meditation and a profound means of changing consciousness and moving through the many different levels between earth and heaven.

The act of breathing is closely linked to the air element of, so you can use breathing exercises as an aid to attune to the AIR angels. This attuncment works especially powerfully when done outside, and obviously feels quite different when the breeze is gentle or you are outside in the midst of a strong wind!

Using the affirmations which follow can bring an awareness of these angels:

> With each outbreath I let go and trust...
>
> With each inbreath I receive God's wisdom into every cell of my being.
>
> I feel compassion for all in need.
>
> My heart and mind are open in brotherhood to all life.

Key Words to help focus attunement to the angelic Air vibration

Creative   Wise   Flowing   Understanding   Thoughtful   Positive
Harmonising   Reflective   Aspiring   Detached   Trusting   Energising

Air Angelic Qualities

Inspiration   Energy   Flight   Upliftment   All-encompassing   Enfolding

Key Saying:

'The lesson of the air element
is to bring true understanding of the brotherhood of the Spirit
and that the higher mind should take possession of
and become the ruler of the pupil's thoughts.'

Joan Hodgson

As you tune-in to this energy, write down any affirmations of your own and use the following pages to record your own notes and meditations.

'When a soul has learnt the lesson of Air—learnt brotherhood,
it is ready to share everything with humanity.'

23

'With the inner hearing, you will hear the great Word of Power,
the Creative Word pervading the air.'

'The air element can produce a truly creative and receptive soul.' 25

'The object of the Air Initiation is for the higher mind to be the ruler of your thoughts.'

'With the Air initiation you are learning discernment.'

'The higher mind will never mislead.'

'The higher mind enables the soul to give out of pure love for its brother.'

WATER

Angels of the WATER element are linked not just to the physical element water, but to the soul of humanity and the emotions. The soul lesson of the water element is PEACE and this is the great gift that attunement to these angels can bring. Think of water in all its many manifestations, from the great waves of the ocean to the still waters of a tranquil lake. These very different images demonstrate the great power and variety of this element. Contemplate these as a symbol of human emotions, both their power and the necessity to become master of them rather than be mastered by them.

Angels of the water element can manifest in as many different ways as the physical element water, and the great gift they can bring us is the power to master our emotions and manifest peace in our lives.

✡

Using the affirmations which follow can bring an awareness of these angels:

> I rest at peace in God's heart.
>
> My mind is tranquil; my feelings are in my control.
>
> Peace fills every cell of my being;
> I breathe out peace to all.
>
> I seek to understand and have compassion for all points of view.

30

Key Words to Facilitate Attunement to the Angelic Water Vibration

Flowing   Tolerant   Understanding   Cleansing
Changing   Reflecting   Peaceful   Sensitive   Accepting

Water Angelic Qualities

Peace   Tolerance   Power   Constancy   Reflecting   Stillness

Key Saying:

'As the still water reflects the sky,
so the calm soul reflects the image of God.
When the soul learns to remain tranquil and at peace like a still lake,
it will reflect accurately the truth of the heavens.'

Joan Hodgson

As you tune-in to this energy, write down any affirmations of your own and use the following pages to record your own notes and meditations.

'Water is the symbol of the soul, the psyche;
it possesses a special spiritual vibration. Water is the great life-giver.'

31

'You learn, through the Water initiation, the meaning of being still:
of tranquillity under all conditions.'

'Psychic contact, if it is to be of spiritual value to you, must be controlled by the Christ Spirit.' 33

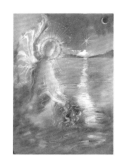

'Water is a purifier of the soul.'

'Have courage to face the truth and you will then pass the Water Initiation.'

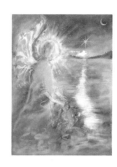

'Learn to balance the emotions,
then they do not stand in the way of the activity of the spirit—the Christ within.'

'Water purifies and cleanses the aura.'

CARDINAL

Key Words for Cardinal Angelic Energy

Dynamic Power   Will   Discipline   Action   Creativity   Joy

The zodiac angels of the cardinal signs come strongly under the ray of the great angels of power and the 'Father' energy, which causes all life to manifest. They are linked with the energy of divine will and bring a feeling of outgoing action—a moving forward, a feeling of creativity and new things. They also bring a great feeling of discipline and one-pointedness, of security, strength and knowledge that God is the all-powerful worker of miracles. In nature, the cardinal signs all come at the start of a new season, bringing the feeling of the power to create and achieve. Cardinal energy angels are vast, taller than the tallest tree, or great streams of water such as the Niagara Falls. Their energy is ever-moving, but powerful and disciplined.

VISUALISATION IDEAS FOR CARDINAL ENERGY ATTUNEMENT

Tune in to the cardinal, outgoing, revitalizing energy. . Breathe it into your whole being, and breathe out old, static, faded energy. Feel the glory of the sun shining down on you. …. then. …. consciously link with the great cardinal energy angels. Breathe their energy into every cell of your being and into each area of your body in turn.

PHYSICAL BODY

First breathe the cardinal, creative energy (like the sun) into your own physical body. Visualise it flowing down through the soles of your feet into the earth. It doesn't matter whether you are wearing shoes, or whether you are indoors or outdoors. Visualise the energy passing right down through all physical things into the earth beneath, eventually touching the 'inner core' of the country in which you are at that time. See this bright cardinal energy helping bring about a deep inner healing and re-awakening the spiritual light in the very heart of this country.

EMOTIONAL BODY

Tune in to the great cardinal angels. Breathe their revitalising energy into your emotional body. It will recharge your spirit and help you release your true creativity. Feel this bubbling up within you like a little spring which has suddenly come to life. ..... . then, allow it to become a glorious fountain. Visualise the cardinal energy cleansing and recharging with God's light all the waters of the world.

MENTAL BODY

Breathe the cardinal energy into your mental body. It will help clear your mind of old thought patterns and open your mind to new enlightenment and inspiration from heaven.

SPIRITUAL SELF

Cardinal angels feel closely linked to the fire element. Breathe their powerful energy into every cell and imagine each breath is connecting you more strongly with your spiritual being until it feels as though there is no separation between your physical self and your spiritual self. It is as though you are a shining star of light (symbolically the upward pointing 'triangle' of your aspiring everyday self is integrated with the downward pointing 'triangle' of your spirit, creating a radiant six-pointed star of light).

Affirmations for aiding attunement to cardinal angels:

I am Divine Power.

I am Divine Joy.

I am Divine Creativity.

I am Divine Inspiration.

As you attune to this energy, write down any affirmations of your own and use the following pages to record your own notes and meditations.

'God is the light; in God we live and without God we have no life at all.'

'Love is a creative force.'

'Form … Colour … Sound … Vibration. All these contain the white magical creative force.' 41

'You can draw to yourself the creative forces,
and utilise them for the gradual perfecting and growth of all forms of life.'

'There is coming a transmutation of the creative forces in the human
from the lower to the higher centres.'

'When you are attuned to the divine creative force, you know true happiness.'

'Bring into operation within your being all the divine laws.'

FIXED

Key Words for Fixed Energy

Stable   Nurturing   Loving   Caring   Building   Maintaining and sustaining

The zodiac angels of fixed signs are very still and steady. They are also vast, but a good analogy for them would be the great temples of stone such as Stonehenge, and cathedral spires. Fixed signs in nature come when the season is well established. The fixed energy brings into manifestation on the earth the beauty of God in each of the elements. The angels are linked with the great impulse of love, and show God's love taking form in the womb of life. Coming into the aura of an angel of one of the fixed signs brings a great feeling of peace and stability, of safeness and nurture—of Mother God. It can bring a real awakening in the soul of absolute unconditional love and an end to narrow, judgmental ways of thought.

VISUALISATION IDEAS FOR FIXED ENERGY ATTUNEMENT

Imagine the beauty of the full moon shining in a clear sky just before dawn. The indigo night still enfolds the earth like a great cloak bringing a feeling of Divine Mother's protective, nurturing energy. Rest in this feeling of being enfolded and nurtured in a warm, loving, protective aura. It may feel as though you sink right down into the earth and become one with its warm heart. You may feel the heart beat. As you become attuned to this rhythmic beat you may start to feel more deeply your link with all aspects of creation...all things created out of earth matter... a feeling of all life enfolded in the love of the mother aspect of God. In this vibration of oneness you are aware of the perfection of the divine plan, which takes care of all.
As the moon sets, the dawn breaks and all the loveliness of nature is revealed in the golden glow of a new day.

Meditate each day on the beauty of

the EARTH, all creatures and their habitats, all the natural world, see all in harmony

the AIR, see it pure and protective around us all

the WATER, see it clean and rich with life

the SUN, see it in all its radiant glory, and behind it the spiritual sun

Affirmations for aiding attunement to fixed angels:

I am Divine Love.

I am Divine Strength.

I am Divine Intuition.

I am Divine Peace.

As you attune to this energy, write down any affirmations of your own and use the following pages to record your own notes and meditations.

'In the four fixed signs you have the base of the pyramid,
the ancient symbol of the whole of the world's life.'

47

'The four fixed signs indicate the completion of the soul's evolution.'

'Do not force yourself, but you will attain your object by patient perseverance.'

'Get it firmly established in your consciousness that you are primarily spirit and not body.
Act by the spirit.'

'Keep mind and heart fixed steadily upon the one source and the truth of life—God.'

'With your vision fixed upon the spiritual goal,
you will acquire a different mental and emotional attitude.'

'Find the place of contact wherein the divine Will can be heard.'

MUTABLE

Key Words for Mutable Angelic Energy

Flowing Understanding Adaptability Tolerance Gentleness

The zodiac angels of the mutable signs have a gentle, flowing energy. Coming into contact with them is like being enfolded in flowing wings or touched by ever-moving, gentle breezes. They bring a feeling of flexibility, movement and change, and all the mutable signs come at a time when nature is flowing from one season to the next. The angels of this mutable quality are linked with divine wisdom, so coming into the aura of an angel of one of the mutable signs brings about an awakening of the higher mind and can help the inner self lift the earthly mind above the confusion and negativity of material things to the higher consciousness of the spirit. This energy also helps unfold a gentle tolerance and understanding of the many ways of being, the many pathways to an awareness and trust in God. Acceptance is one of the key qualities of the mutable signs—the ability to go with the flow of life and to trust in the divine plan.

VISUALISATION IDEAS FOR MUTABLE ENERGY ATTUNEMENT

Close your eyes and open your whole intuitive being to the ever-moving, ever-flowing energy of the mutable angels. Tune in to this vibration within all four natural elements. These angels manifest divine wisdom. Tuning in to their vibration helps open the earthly mind to much deeper understanding of God's great plan for the evolution of all life, and of our planet earth.

EARTH

Imagine yourself becoming one with the ever-moving leaves of a great tree on a windy day, or the pebbles on a beach, in constant motion caused by the flow and ebb of the tide, or feel yourself become a flower which has passed its full maturity and is changing in form to bring forth fruit. …. Relax, flow, change and deepen your understanding of God's wisdom in your life. All things change except God's eternal love for all creation. Our security lies in God's love and care for us no matter what happens in life—release your body with trust into this moment, and the next and the next...

WATER

Imagine yourself becoming one with the ever-moving water of a river or the waves of the sea, or sit by moving water and watch the many changing images of light and shade. Allow these images to help you surrender your will to God's will. Release all feelings from the past into the stream of water and become at peace with the ever-moving flow.

AIR

Imagine you are flying through the air (kite surfing or hang gliding, maybe!). Enjoy the feel of air flowing all over your body and the feeling of freedom. Through these feelings you may let go of past habits of thought, allow them to drop away from your mind as you soar above their limitations. Your mind is empty of all that held you back; open to new ideas and freedom from fear.

FIRE

Imagine yourself enjoying the glorious warmth of the sun, or a blazing bonfire on a cold day and being able to dance freely in the flames without being burnt. The fiery flames consume all heaviness and old conditions and set you free to fully embrace God's power and creativity flowing into every cell of your being.

Affirmations for aiding attunement to mutable angels:

I am Divine Wisdom.

I am Divine Adaptability.

I am Divine Tolerance.

I am Divine Acceptance.

As you tune-in to this energy, write down any affirmations of your own and use the following pages to record your own notes and meditations.

'Become at-one with universal life, the act of the dewdrop merging into the ocean.'

'We say to you take step by step whatever is open to you. Just go with the tide'

'Do not think because a door closes that another does not open.
You pass from one condition of life to another.'

'Good, or love, is the flowing out, the giving out.'

'With the fuller consciousness there will be a change in the physical body.
a development of the body of light.'

60 'We open to the river of life from God and its flowing back once more—the completed circle.'

'Open your being to the vibrations of love and wisdom
flowing continually from the heart of the universe.'

ARIES

Cardinal Fire
SOUL LESSON:

Positive Key Words for Aries: Outgoing, Pioneering, Innovative.

Planetary Angel Influences: Mars and Sun

Aries is the first sign of the zodiac and has a strongly innovative and pioneering feel. This comes from both the cardinal and the fire energy. Before you start to attune to the Aries angelic influence, you may like to look at the sections for both CARDINAL and FIRE.

The soul lesson of Aries is Love in Action. The Aries zodiac angels manifest a radiant, brilliant, creative, transformational light. Think of bright orange/gold fiery flames reaching from earth to sky. All old clutter and waste is burned away in the cleansing fire, making way for a new start. Aries angels are like huge powerful flames, but they are not something to fear, for they radiate absolute unconditional love.

Use these ARIES affirmations to help you attune to this angelic energy:

> I open myself to angelic power and creativity.
> My heart is open to heavenly inspiration.
> The light of God's love radiates upon me and within me.

Using ARIES angelic energy in your everyday life

Aries is the first sign of the zodiac, therefore it can be really helpful to tune in to the Aries angelic energy if you want to make a new start in one area of your life, or if you want to begin a new creative project:

* Inwardly ask for the help of Aries angels.
* Tune in to their ray of bright, creative inspiration.
* Write down any ideas which come.
* If you doubt your own ability, feel the hopeful, positive energy of the Aries angels lifting you up.

'Your light shines; you are seen from far distances; and are used to do constructive work.'   63

64   'The answer is in the heart, and manifests a spontaneous reaction to life—kindness.'

'Love finds its greatest expression in silent ministration or giving forth.' 65

66   'A moment will come when your kind action will be recalled. No kindness or love is ever lost.'

'You are learning to comprehend light as a manifestation of love in human action.'   67

'That which is good is creative, and it lives and it acts in due time.'

'What you are in your heart is reflected in your words and in your life.'

TAURUS

Fixed Earth

SOUL LESSON

SERVICE through LOVE

Positive Key Words for Taurus: Practical, Well-grounded, Peaceful

Planetary Angel Influences: **Venus** and **Moon**

Taurus is a Fixed Earth sign, so before you attune to the Taurus angelic influence, look at the sections for FIXED and EARTH.

The soul lesson of Taurus is Service through Love. The Taurean zodiac angels manifest a glorious heart-opening vibration of God's pure, unconditional love for all life, from the smallest single-celled creature to the largest tree and mammal. They also bring a deep dedicated ray of service. As the human heart is touched and opened by God's love, there follows the deep desire to give the life in service to creation. The vibration of the sun in Taurus also brings a feeling for creating beauty.

Use these TAURUS affirmations to help you attune to this angelic energy:

> I open my heart in love for all creation.
>
> I work to serve and nurture all.
>
> I am a creator of beauty.

Using TAURUS angelic energy in your everyday life

Tuning in to Taurean angelic energy will help you create beauty and harmony in your physical environment. Use this help when you are arranging beautiful things around you in your home, creating a lovely meal, or working in your garden. Also remember your own physical temple—your body—and give it loving attention and nurture, for example a relaxing bath, beauty treatment or walk in the countryside... As you do this, feel the gentle enfoldment of the angels...open your whole being to their influence. Even if you do not live in beautiful surroundings, you can tune in to the Taurean angelic energy to create beauty and harmony at an inner level. Visualise the beauty for which you long. Play soothing music and burn incense to bring the angelic harmony closer. As you create this inner beauty and harmony, so you will be able to pass it on to all around you.

'It is the Light in all things which reveals beauty to us.'

'If you act from the heart of love towards others, you have nothing to fear
no matter what the circumstances.'

'Love means giving.
When you love you have the emotion of flowing out in order to help, to serve.'

74   'Love God faithfully, and by the power of this light miracles can be wrought, healing performed.'

'Love is a magical principle, worker of wonders. Use love rightly and it has a remarkable effect.' 75

'As your heart centre opens in love and kindness towards your fellow creatures,
it begins to expand.'

'Act from the heart of love,
put the divine law into practice, and you may have confidence that all will be well.' 77

GEMINI

Mutable Air

SOUL LESSON

Brotherhood through Wisdom

Positive Key Words for GEMINI: **Quick-witted, Communicative, Flexible**

Planetary Angel Influence: **Mercury**

Before you start to attune to the Gemini angelic influence, look at the sections for MUTABLE and AIR.

The soul lesson of Gemini is Brotherhood through Wisdom. All mutable signs have a link with the planets which rule communication and for Gemini it is Mercury. The mercurial influence is really strong in Gemini, and as you tune into the Geminian angels you will probably automatically link with the quicksilver, intuitive energy of this planet. A challenge for Gemini (and linking with Geminian angels!) is to keep still and focused enough to absorb the true wisdom of heaven, before getting diverted onto the next fascinating mental pursuit.

Use these GEMINI affirmations to help you attune to this angelic energy:

Using GEMINI angelic energy in your everyday life

> I open my mind to angelic inspiration.
> Angels guide and focus my thought.
> I use my mind for good in the world.

Pray that the Geminian angels will help you in all your communication with those around you—family, colleagues, friends and the wider community. Visualise the shining light of the six-pointed star filling your mind with heavenly wisdom and clearer understanding, so that all you say and do will be truly wise and loving. If there is a particular situation in your life which is causing concern at this time, lovingly offer it to the Geminian angels to help to awaken your understanding of the outworking of God's plan and bring you new inspiration to help or resolve the difficulties.

The Gemini angelic influence is linked with communication of every kind. Attune to this vibration to aid clarity and focus in your communications. Decide on a form of communication you enjoy using, for example e-mail, telephone, text or letter, and communicate with someone with whom you have not been in touch for a while, who may be lonely or in need of support.

'The outpouring of the Christ life is powerful in the sign of Gemini.'

'Humanity will come to realise that all creation is one vast brotherhood of spirit,
one atom inseparable from another.'

'Apparent injustice can be turned into a jewel in your temple, revealing the divinest truths.'

'See truly and you pass between the pillars of the higher and the lower mind;
there is absolute balance.'

'To love you must be wise;
you can give the greatest amount of help to others by wisdom as well as by love.'

84   'It is the actual experience of living with others which enables you to gain wisdom.'

'By sincere aspiration and wisdom you can turn all into beauty and peace and happiness.'   85

CANCER  Cardinal Water

Peace in Action

SOUL LESSON

Positive Key Words for CANCER: Sensitive, Nurturing, Home-loving.

Planetary Angel Influence: **Moon**

Before you start to attune to the Cancer angelic influence, look at the sections for CARDINAL and WATER.

The deep soul lesson of Cancer is Peace through Action. As it is a cardinal sign it brings a feeling of moving forward into a fresh period and a time to look at things with new eyes. This time for clear reflection can bring greater peace, harmony and wellbeing into your life. Cancer also brings a feminine feeling of the Mother aspect of the Creator. It is a time to meditate on Divine Mother and pray for a further awakening of her intuitive qualities deep within the innermost being. This applies to all of us, men as well as women!

Use these CANCER affirmations to help you attune to this angelic energy:

> I breathe in peace and inspiration.
> I breathe out anxiety and restless thoughts.
> Angels create my inner sanctuary of peace.

Using CANCER angelic energy in your everyday life

Whatever the environment in which you live, Cancer angelic energy can help you create greater peace and beauty in your surroundings. Consciously ask for angelic help to do this. Breathe in the angelic vibration. .... breathe out and affirm peace.

Create one little area which becomes a sanctuary for you, using things such as candles, flowers and incense if these help. Then turn within to contact your inner home or temple, your place of peace. If you are frightened or worried about anything, imagine angels enfolding you in their protective aura of light.

'At the full moon, the silver moon, which the ancients regarded as the symbol of the higher mind, there comes a hush of quiet waiting.'

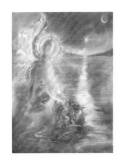

'Action is good at the right time,
especially action as the result of meditation and prayer, and not of emotional stress.'

'Put peace into action in your daily life and it must slowly penetrate national and international life.' 89

'The only way, the key to all action on earth is love, is kindness, gentleness.'

'Your innermost centre is the basis of all action—
from this centre you can receive an answer to every problem.'

'You will find that your ability to act grows more perfect when you are still within.'

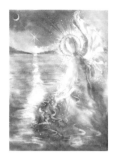

'By strengthening the spirit within you, you will find yourself living with greater precision.' 93

LEO

Fixed Fire

Love

SOUL LESSON

Positive Key Words for LEO:

Warm-hearted, Loving, Confident

Planetary Angel Influence:

Sun

Leo is a Fixed Fire sign. Before you start to attune to the Leo angelic influence, look at the sections for FIRE and FIXED.

The soul lesson for Leo is Love. Leo angels are like the sun and meditation with them often feels like resting in the heart of the sun. There is a gentle feeling too, almost like resting in petals, in the soft heart of a rose.
Leo brings the radiant, warm, positive energy of sunshine, and has a strong link with masculine, outgoing energy. However, it also brings the softer, nurturing, enfolding energy of the feminine aspect of life as its soul lesson is LOVE.

Use these LEO affirmations to help you attune to this angelic energy:

<u>Using LEO angelic energy in your everyday life</u>

Attuning to Leo angelic energy can help a great deal if you are feeling any lack in your life. .... lack of love or resources of any kind. Just think of the Sun shining down on you and breathe the sunlight into every cell of your body. Relax and 'sun bathe'. .... Imagine you are resting in angels' wings!

> I open my heart to abundant love, and give.
> Angelic beings bathe me in heavenly sunlight.
> I rest in God's heart.

Attuning to the dynamic aspect of Leo angelic energy will help you radiate joy and wellbeing to all those around you, and inspire and uplift everyone you contact.

LEO angelic attunement
(for your meditation notes, visualisations and affirmations)

'Attune yourself to the first great cause—the Sun;
become in harmony with the Sun and with the light.'

'Have absolute confidence in God's love.

Know that all things lead you to a greater understanding of God's love.'

'Love is the fire, a great life force. On this vibration we find magic.'

'Open your heart and mind in confidence of God.'

'The key to all knowledge is in the heart—the simple key of love.'

'When love fills the heart, the heart centre burns and radiates like the sun.'

'This is the magical secret of the initiate's life, the transmuting power of love.' 101

VIRGO

Mutable Earth

SOUL LESSON

Careful, Precise, Conscientious

Mercury

Service through Wisdom

Positive Key Words for VIRGO:

Planetary Angel Influence:

Before you start to attune to the Virgo angelic influence, look at the sections for EARTH and MUTABLE.
The soul lesson of Virgo is Service through Wisdom. Virgo angels are incredibly beautiful with an infinite variety of soft swirling pearly colours. They come closely under the aura of Divine Mother—the mother aspect of the creator of all life—and particularly manifest her wise understanding of the need of and care for every single aspect of created life. The energy of Virgo helps encourage knowledge of all the aspects of God's plan as it is earthed in form, in created life.

The Virgo angelic energy helps care for all the intricate details of God's perfect plan for life on earth. God's wisdom is so great we cannot really comprehend it with our physical brains.

Use these VIRGO affirmations to help you attune to this angelic energy:

<u>Using VIRGO angelic energy in your everyday life</u>

> I trust in God's angels and the plan for my life.
> I release all tension and open my heart to the angels of wisdom.
> Angels guide me on my path of service.

Tune in to Virgo angelic energy to help you calm down your earthly mind, which may worry a great deal about small details of God's plan for your life, your loved ones, or the world. Take several slow deep breaths and surrender all your worries back to God. Breathe in the absolute realisation that God's plan IS perfect.
Make a plan for a new dietary regime (if you need this), a more relaxed stress-free programme—or whatever is right for you. Then think about your work and service in the world. Contemplate how you might make changes and adjustments which will enable you to work and serve more productively and at the same time ensure plenty of rest, nurture and re-creation for you. Ask the Virgo angels to help you with this.

'Those who miss what they long for on earth can be quite sure that their ideal will manifest.
There is nothing truer. And this should be an assurance, a comfort, a star to follow.'

'With the gaining of wisdom and understanding through love,
we come into the full power of our creation.'

'The angels of Saturn bring wisdom through human experience,
strength of character, and a deep patience.'

106 'Love is power, and must be used with wisdom. This is why love and wisdom become one ray.'

'Let your motive for seeking wisdom be to better equip yourself for God's service
and to relieve suffering.'

108   'With the incoming of Light, must come a desire to give succour and joy to other people.'

'God's plan is to bring beauty—
not perfection, not in the limited sense in which the word is understood.'

LIBRA Cardinal Air

SOUL LESSON

Brotherhood through Action

Positive Key Words for LIBRA: **Sociable, Harmonising, Beauty-Loving**

Planetary Angel Influences: **Venus and Saturn**

Before you start to attune to the Libran angelic influence, look at the sections for AIR and CARDINAL.

Libra's soul lesson is Brotherhood through Action. The vibrations of the angels of Libra bring a feeling for beauty and harmony and of balance between heaven and earth. There is a blend of strong Saturnian energy and the gentle, softer Venusian influence. These two different energies can sometimes at an earthly level lead to indecision, and a desire for harmony at all costs. It is therefore helpful to use the Libran angelic influence to bring about a wise balancing of these energies.

Use these LIBRAN affirmations to help you attune to this angelic energy:

The angels help me to be poised and maintain balance.
The angels of beauty draw close.
I am helped to find harmonious solutions.

Using LIBRAN angelic energy in your everyday life

Think about your partner, close colleagues, friends or relatives, and make a list of ways in which you could create greater harmony and wellbeing between you. Then, thinking of your own life, assess if you have a good balance between work and recreation, physical and spiritual pursuits, your own thoughts and what others think. Decide if there is anything you need to do to balance your life better. Then tune in to the Libran angelic energy to help you act on your thoughts in the most productive and decisive way you can.

Again, tuning in to the Libran angelic energy, visualise yourself and your partner (or closest friend/relative/colleague) enjoying a wonderful day out together in one of your favourite places in nature. Imagine all the happiness you can share in a time of loving harmony, when any differences, misunderstandings melt away in the Libran energy of beauty, harmony and wellbeing.

LIBRA angelic attunement
(for your meditation notes, visualisations and affirmations)

'We mean by good, the continual working for equilibrium, the power of holding a balance.'

'You have the strength and confidence to put truth into action.'

'Try to understand the motive behind another's action,
and not to assume that the motive is unkind.'

'Brotherhood—gentleness in speech, truth in action—
the unmistakeable signs of the true and the beautiful.'

'As the higher mind functioning behind the scenes becomes strong
it directs every thought and action.'

'Wisdom is a part of love. Therefore in action you need to be wise.'

'There is no separation between angels and people; they work together side by side.'

SCORPIO

Fixed Water

SOUL LESSON

Peace through Love

Positive Key Words for SCORPIO: Deep thinking, Quiet, Intuitive

Planetary Angel Influences: Mars and Pluto

Before you start to attune to the Scorpio angelic influence, look at the sections for FIXED and WATER.

The soul lesson of Scorpio is Peace through Love. Astrologically, Scorpio brings a connection with the fundamental issues of birth and death, sex, and deep hidden feelings. Its ruling planet is Mars and so there is a fiery aspect to this sign; the divine fire which creates new life, new ideas and aspirations from the deepest depths to the highest heights.

The vibration of the great zodiac angels of Scorpio is very powerful indeed. The more limited aspect of Scorpio is symbolised by the scorpion, whilst the aspirational symbol is the powerful eagle, soaring into the sky.

Use these SCORPIO affirmations to help you attune to this angelic energy:

<u>Using SCORPIO angelic energy in your everyday life</u>

The Scorpio angelic energy will help you tune into your deepest creative energy and driving life-force. When

> I trust in the process of transformation and growth.
>
> The angels lift me up.
>
> Love is eternal; nothing is ever lost.

you feel weak, lifeless, unwell or unable to cope with difficult circumstances in your life, as we all do from time to time, consciously call on the help of the Scorpio angels. Visualise the sun shining brightly overhead (do this outside if circumstances permit). Relax in the healing, re-energising light of the sun, and allow all your weakness to melt away. Then, breathe in the life-force of the sun. Feel it igniting the life that is buried deep within your own being.

Reflect on deeply significant moments in your life which may well be concerned with death of loved ones or big changes. Some will have had a most powerful effect on you. Ask the Scorpio angels to help you find inner peace, through understanding more about the meaning of life and the eternal nature of true love.

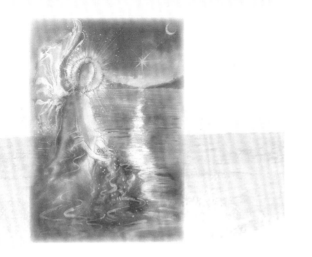

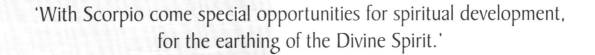

'With Scorpio come special opportunities for spiritual development,
for the earthing of the Divine Spirit.'

'Visualise the lotus flower on the still water.'

'Meditate on love and you will be changed—
you will know what it means to be happy; to be at peace.'

'Angels will bring you a ray of light and knowledge
which will teach you how to rise, how to develop your wings.'

'Sensitiveness can result from an increase in spiritual power...
but endeavour to attain and maintain an even and still vibration.'

124   'Cultivate compassion and tenderness, tolerance and patience with others. That is real love.'

'If you want to be loved, radiate love.
As soon as this is realised peace comes.'

SAGITTARIUS

Mutable Fire

SOUL LESSON

Positive Key Words for SAGITTARIUS: Encouraging, Aspirational, Expansive

Planetary Angel Influence: Jupiter

Sagittarius is a Mutable Fire sign, so before you start to attune to the Sagittarian angelic influence, look at the sections for MUTABLE and FIRE.

The soul lesson of Sagittarius is Love through Wisdom. Sagittarius zodiac angels can manifest as ever-moving, brilliant flames of light, leaping heavenward, then dying down and almost disappearing before returning with increased vigour.

In tuning-in to these angels the power and energy of the fire element is experienced in its mutable phase, bringing a feeling of movement, change and making way for new inspiration. This angelic vibration brings a glorious impulse of aspiration to God and heavenly things. The ruling planet is Jupiter, planet of the higher mind, religion and expansion of consciousness.

Use these SAGITTARIUS affirmations to help you attune to this angelic energy:

Using SAGITTARIUS angelic energy in your everyday life

> I expand my consciousness and become free.
>
> Angels of love inspire me and raise me up.
>
> Creativity and inspiration flow to me from the heart of the sun.

Outside (or visualising being there), consciously breathe God's healing light into every cell of your physical body and see the cells becoming re-energised and renewed. Particularly visualise your blood stream cleansed by the light and flowing to every cell, to nurture, renew and bring new life. As you do this, attune to the Sagittarian angels and feel their vibrant life force almost giving you wings, so you feel you could fly! If there are areas in your life where you feel held down, burdened or restricted, ask the Sagittarian angels to help you set yourself free inwardly. Many restrictions and burdens can be lightened by the way we view them. Ask for help in creating a new perspective as you inwardly fly free on wings of light, gaining a new view of your life.

'Think of shining, apparently winged beings, moving in the heavens into light and more light,
with greater freedom and greater and greater comprehension of this universe
and of universes beyond this small universe.'

'Those who choose the path of love and wisdom reach the goal
by finding that one true light, the eternal flame.'

'You are far safer to follow the path of love even if you make mistakes.'

'Seek knowledge—and wisdom to interpret that knowledge.'

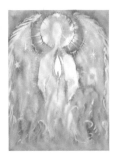

'One of the most precious gifts of life is wisdom, through love.'

'The heart does not register incorrectly; that which the heart absorbs is truth.'

'Love and wisdom go hand in hand; the ungoverned emotions of love can be harmful.'

CAPRICORN

Cardinal Earth

SOUL LESSON

Positive Key Words for CAPRICORN: **Patient, Realistic, Hard-working**

Planetary Angel Influences: **Saturn and Mars**

Before you start to attune to the Capricornian angelic influence, look at the sections for CARDINAL and EARTH.

The soul lesson of Capricorn is Service through Action. The Capricorn zodiac angels manifest a strong, steady but vibrant energy. They bring a great feeling of discipline and determination. As you come into their aura you may immediately feel a little taller and stronger and experience a new surge of energy and determination to fulfil all the tasks you have set yourself. New clarity will come too, you will know what is now truly important and what you can discard and let fall away like a tree shedding its old leaves making way for fresh growth.

Use these CAPRICORN affirmations to help you attune to this angelic energy:

Using CAPRICORN angelic energy in your everyday life

> I access my full potential in all areas of life.
> The angels bring me strength and focus.
> I flow with the moment and serve with joy.

Capricorn energy can aid positive and helpful reflection on the past. Attune to the Capricorn angels as you reflect on past relationships which may need healing or forgiveness. Also reflect on the spiritual lessons arising from past events and note what you feel you have understood better, and where letting go and moving on might be helpful. Reflect on all the opportunities you have taken to be of service to those around you. As you link with the energy of Capricorn angels breathe in their strength, courage and encouragement to achieve what your soul needs for this lifetime. Think about this in the everyday and longer term. How does your soul growth manifest in your career, your relationships and in your service to others? Write this down and make conscious decisions about how you would like this to develop.

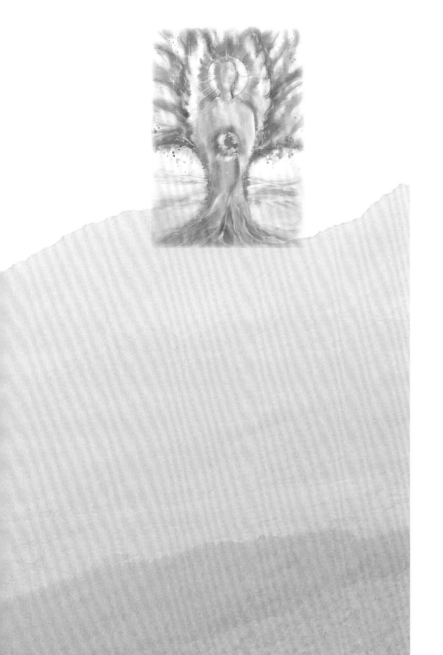

'Beautiful things are created by strong, steady vibrations.'

'Every action brings its due reward, brings its due result.'

'Spiritual aspiration sometimes means service, action,
and through action the soul grows in stature.'

137

'Living rightly means attuning to infinite love and wisdom,
you are then bringing it into every word and action.'

'Right action is God action.'

'Peace on earth, brotherhood and the cessation of war and conflict is bound to come with your right action.'

'As you put the Law of God into action in your life, you will be fulfilled.'

AQUARIUS

Fixed Air

SOUL LESSON

Positive Key Words for AQUARIUS: **Friendly, Objective, Fair-minded**

Planetary Angel Influences: **Saturn and Uranus**

Before you attune to the Aquarian angelic influence, look at the sections for FIXED and AIR.

The soul lesson of the Sun in Aquarius is Brotherhood through Love. The Aquarian angelic energy certainly brings a strong feeling for the brotherhood of all life and will help establish in the new Aquarian Age, a way of life on earth which is more fair, tolerant and balanced than the previous age. Inflexible, separative and judgemental ways of thought will melt away as both mind and heart of humankind are touched by the Aquarian influence and the awakening, transformative, lightning-flash of Uranus, which is co-ruler of this sign with Saturn. The planet Saturn is often misunderstood: its influence is not necessarily heavy. It brings a great sense of responsibility, with an ability for hard work. Aquarian energy is strong, sensible and enduring (it is a fixed sign!).

Use these AQUARIAN affirmations to help you attune to this angelic energy:

> The angels inspire true brotherhood in me.
> I serve with compassion through stillness.
> I look on life with a kindly humour.

<u>Using AQUARIAN angelic energy in your everyday life</u>

The Aquarian angelic vibration can help awaken deeper understanding of what true brotherhood means. As you tune in to the Aquarian influence, contemplate issues which you find hard to understand, forgive or tolerate. Sometimes it can be very hard to keep the heart open in true, loving understanding when behaviour of others is anti-social, difficult, aggressive, etc. Aquarian angels can help cultivate a broader understanding and truly open heart.

Aquarian angelic inspiration will facilitate brotherhood in action projects and community service. It fosters a wide open-hearted and tolerant understanding of many different cultural and religious viewpoints, and an emotional detachment which can be very helpful.

'Respond to Uranus and find that suddenly there breaks upon your consciousness, understanding ... light.'

'If you feel acutely the effect of the thoughts and actions of others,
learn to consider these wisely and dispassionately.'

'With the dispassionate mind, the higher mind,
we comprehend a Love which both gives and withholds.'

145

'Clear vision means an inward knowing.
With this you know the truth, you recognise the love existent in others.'

'Thought creates good, thought can heal.'

'Cultivate the art of loving others.'

'Don't be afraid to trust in the power of love,
love is the dynamic force which brought life to the world.'

PISCES

Mutable Water
SOUL LESSON

Peace through Wisdom

Positive Key Words for PISCES: Sensitive, Visionary, Empathetic

Planetary Angel Influences: **Jupiter and Neptune**

Before you start to attune to the Piscean angelic influence, look at the sections for MUTABLE and WATER.

The soul lesson of Pisces is Peace through Wisdom. The Piscean angelic energy brings an extremely gentle, sensitive and sympathetic vibration. Connecting with this energy helps awaken the intuitive wisdom of the 'mind in the heart'.
The ruling planet of Pisces is Jupiter, the planet of the higher mind and expansion of consciousness. The great zodiac angels of Pisces come strongly under this Jupiterian influence, but there is also a Neptunian connection. Neptune has a dual influence, being a planet of spiritual illumination but also of muddle and confusion. This can bring a feeling either of being lost in a maze or of swimming freely in the sunlit waters of a lake of peace, looking up at the light of a clear sky.

Use these PISCES affirmations to help you attune to this angelic energy:

Using PISCES angelic energy in your everyday life

Piscean angelic energy aids intuitive awareness of conditions and other people's needs, but it can bring oversensitivity.

> I am centred and still—the angels draw close.
> Trust brings me strength.
> My heart radiates peace and healing to all.

Think about your life and whether you are allowing yourself to be too much affected by other people's thoughts and opinions. Tune in to Piscean angels to help you keep centred in your own inner power and wisdom. Piscean angelic energy will help you to empathise with others when you are finding it difficult to understand how they are feeling. Breathe in the gentle, understanding energy of Pisces; breathe out any rigid thoughts or feelings, so that you can listen to other people's thoughts and opinions but also maintain your own truth. Consciously let go of old energy, and breathe in new. With every breath feel and see this new energy circulating in and around your body. Feel yourself becoming a new being—refreshed, re-energised.

150

'Pisces brings love and emotion,
and the soul responds to the pure ray of love from the Christ heart.'

'It is necessary to distinguish between love which is wisdom,
and emotionalism which may disintegrate love.'

'Pray for the peace of the ages, of the eternal wisdom, which knows no fear, nothing but God.' 153

'Love and wisdom produce divine Peace.'

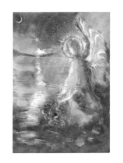

'Your heart is loving, but that is not enough by itself.
You must strive for poise, inner strength and wisdom.'

'The gentle Master knows. He will give you the wisdom to act rightly.'

'Touch that degree of tranquillity which brings humility,
then you will see far beyond the limitations of the mind.'

A Meditation in the Heavenly Astrological Star Temple

Visualise a glorious, blazing six-pointed Star shining down on you from a clear night sky. See a bright ray of light from the Star reaching down towards you, forming a stairway of light to heavenly places. With your guide at your side, feel yourself climbing up the stairway, breathing in the starlight to give you energy and lift you upwards.

As you reach the Star, imagine the form of a crystal temple within the Star. There are twelve steps with a zodiac symbol on each. Planetary symbols are on the entrance pillars. The doorway is itself a bright golden star. As you approach, the door opens and you enter a vast circular arena. As your inner eyes adjust to the light, colour and movement, you become aware of twelve great pillars, or beings of light. These are manifestations of the twelve zodiac vibrations, the great angelic beings representing each of the twelve zodiac signs.

Look to the centre of the circular temple. Here is a huge, clear quartz crystal. It is a perfect (twelve-sided) dodecahedron. It is slowly turning, reflecting the light of the crystal star shining from the centre of the domed roof. As it turns, the light catching the edges of the dodecahedron is split into an infinite variety of shades of glorious colour.

Your guide takes you to stand in the aura of, one of the twelve 'pillars'— your zodiac angel—and standing here you absorb the vibration of this particular angelic energy. Later you may find you are taken around the circle to experience the vibration of the other eleven angels. Or, if you are currently working with one particular angel, stay in the aura of just that one.

When you have completed your time in the temple, your guide will lead you back to earth through a beautiful garden. Sit here for a while, experiencing all four elements, then gently breathe your way right back into your physical body. Complete your meditation by picturing yourself in a protective wigwam of light with a star at the top and see yourself standing at the centre of an equal-sided cross of light surrounded by light. This will ground and protect you.

Further Reading from the White Eagle Publishing Trust:

New Lands • Brewells Lane • Liss • Hampshire • England • GU33 7HY
Tel: 01730 893300 • email: sales@whiteagle.org • www.whiteaglepublishing.org

§

ZODIAC ANGEL WORKBOOK first published August 2008   Text & Images © The White Eagle Publishing Trust 2008

British Library Cataloguing in Publication Data
A Catalogue record for this book is available from the British Library

ISBN 978-0-85487-182-7

Set in 14pt Barrett and 60pt Flapper
Printed and bound in China by Artical Printing